"Hey, Are You Listening?"

Lessons on How God Speaks to Us in Everyday Life.

By:

LaWanda C. Todd

Published by:

Cannon Publishing

"Hey, Are You Listening?"

Lessons on How God Speaks to Us in Everyday Life.

By:

LaWanda C. Todd

Published by:

Cannon Publishing

Hey, Are You Listening? Lessons on How God speaks to us in everyday life.

Printed in the United States of America

Cannon Publishing
P.O. Box 1298
Greenville, NC 27835
888-502-2228
www.cannonpublishing.net

ISBN-13:
978-1537726236

ISBN-10:
1537726234

For information, address: Attention LaWanda C. Todd at lawandatodd@yahoo.com.

Dedication

I dedicate this book to my Mother-in-love, Inez "Ganny" Todd. Your "round mama" is an Author!!!! We miss you. We love you. When the sun is shining bright, we know you are just beyond the clouds smiling. We know you are with us.

Acknowledgements

Obviously, I have to acknowledge Jesus Christ. My rock, My fortress, My deliverer, My God, My strength, My Hightower (Psalms 18:2). Thank you savior for sacrificing your life for me. Thank you for giving me every word that is in this book. Thank you for my story. I love you.

I have to thank two amazing people; Pastors Linwood & Denise Barrett. My pastors and parents. Ma, thanks for finally falling for pops corny pickup lines. Pops, thanks for being persistent in pursuing Ma. I wouldn't be here if you gave up. I love you both. Thank you for always covering me, helping me, praying for me, supporting me and believing in me.

To the best husband in the universe, my big sexy, Terry Todd. You said "I Do" over 18 years ago and I'm so grateful that you still love me in spite of my flaws. You still give me butterflies. Your love and support through this process has carried me. You pulled me through doubts and fears. You saw success and the end result. You see ME. I love you. Thank you.

Tay, Taryn and Eli......my hearts. My babies. My everything's. Thank you for "acting" like I have been a good mom to you. The three of you keep me on toes.... and knees! I love yall and I know without a shadow of a doubt, yall love me too.

Ramon, Latonya, Linwood Jr., Daniel & Darnell - my siblings: Thank you for giving me material to write about for decades to come :) I could not ask for better siblings. Please do not write a tell-all book on the type of sister I have been. I will deny everything. I love each of you and you know this man!!!!

Ok, so I said I was not going to list names because I most likely will forget someone, but I have to acknowledge just a few people. My support system is huge. My circle of friends see my potential long before I see it. They have seen me at my best and my worse and they stayed! Each of you hold a special place in my heart. Cathy, Tee Tee and Rose....there aren't enough pages in this book to thank you for accepting me, loving me and ALWAYS being in my corner for over 20 years. I never once felt like a 4th wheel to an already established trio. Shawn & Tonya, the both of you are so amazing. I have learned so much from the two of you since moving to NC. You are my role models. The individual relationships I have with the two of you are irreplaceable and priceless. I love you both to the gristle bone. Natalie, thank you for always letting me vent with no judgement. I can just be Wanda and you get me. You are my sounding board. Thank you for steering me in the right direction. Chanel, thank you for your friendship, support and loyalty. I can always count on you. That means more to me than you know. Each of you have laughed and cried with me. Each of you corrected me when I was wrong. Each of you encouraged me when I needed it. Thank you.

To my New Faith Deliverance Holiness Ministries family. Yall are the bomb.com. We have grown so much since the church doors opened in 1998. You keep me covered in prayer. I love each of you so very much and thank you for loving me back. The "Sisters Supporting Sisters" crew keeps it real and keeps me on track. I have one biological sister but plenty of "drafted in" sisters that I lean on so much. You know who you are. Thank you.

To my Barrett & Todd Family.....I love each of you. I have the best family in the world. Would not trade any of you....well maybe a handful of you...but I will keep the rest of you. So glad to proudly wear the Barrett and Todd name.

If I didn't acknowledge you in this book, don't fret. There will be more books to follow :)

Hope you enjoy ☺

Peace out Homies,

LaWanda

Foreword

The roar of thunder and crackle of lightening heard in the midst of a storm, the still quiet of the wee hours, a child's laughter, the combined calmness and power of ocean waves and the many lessons from nature and life that we experience every day are just a few of the infinite ways in which our Almighty God speaks, whispers and admonishes us to hear Him, and I mean really *hear* Him!

It has taken some time to get my hearing right, but I've finally learned to listen in many different ways to the beckoning and instruction of the Holy Spirit. I hear Him in prayer, conversations, in my Spirit and through purpose-driven tools like this book. In *Hey, Are You Listening?* LaWanda Todd, brilliantly reminds us of how God truly speaks –as the saying goes - in mysterious ways. Ways sometimes beyond our human conception, but still in ways our Spirit man clearly understands and receives as truth.

The stories she shares are heartfelt and transparent and will take you through a myriad of emotions, as many of them will be familiar to situations you may have experienced. Depending on what season of your life you were in at the time, you may not have been listening very well, so she reminds us of the power of hearing, as she begs the question on each page, *Hey, Are You Listening?*

This book has taken me on a journey of reflection of my life, as it will for you. I have thought back to my poor beginnings in Jamaica. We didn't have much, but we knew God and how to rely on instruction from Him. This hearing was critical when we migrated to the United States with practically no worldly possessions. We didn't have anything most would consider valuable, but we had each other and we knew how to hear from God. As I grew up, this ability to hear guided me through obtaining multiple degrees and eventually led me up the corporate ladder. By trusting, believing and *listening*, I found myself, by the grace of God, as COO and SVP of United Healthcare Provider Network and President and CEO of GE-Clinical Service, Inc the largest bio-medical company in the world. Me, a poor black boy from Jamaica. This was an honor and I served in the role as unto God, but I soon learned that listening doesn't stop when you think you've "made it".

The ability to hear God's lessons and obey His instruction became even more important, when I heard in my spirit that God wanted me to leave a seven-figure income and all that comes with it to pursue ministry full-time and be an entrepreneur for my provision. It's at times like these that we think our ears are clogged. We wonder if we're going deaf and think our mind is playing tricks on us. No, if it's inconceivable in your mind, chances are you've heard clearly from God! That was the case for me! I left it all to pursue a higher and nobler call to minister the word of God in the marketplace as the Senior Pastor & Founder of multiple Kingdom Church ministries across the globe and CEO/Owner of multiple businesses throughout the U.S., I've never looked back or questioned my hearing again!

I want the same for you and so does our Father. He wants you to stay sensitive to His voice and the direction He needs you to take. King Solomon, the wisest man who have ever lived other than Christ, made an amazing statement in his writings in Proverbs 19:21 when he wrote, "many are the plans in a man's heart, but only the purpose of God prevails". Only the Creator knows the purpose of what he has created. He wants you to discover your purpose so badly, that He has authored this book through his vessel, LaWanda Todd, just to ask you one important, destiny-changing question, *Hey, Are You Listening?* This just might be the most important question of your life.

Dale Jones,

Pastor & Entrepreneur

Contents

Introduction

My parents raised me and my siblings in the church. You would think that made me a communications expert when it came to hearing from God. That is not the truth. For many years, I struggled with my identity in Christ because I did not "hear" him as others did. He did not wake me out of my sleep to speak to me. I did not hear a loud strong voice from Heaven giving me directions. I did not have a Prophet at my disposal to consult when I needed an urgent answer from God. Everyone would say, just wait and listen. He will speak. I waited and waited and waited. I heard nothing. This caused some difficulties in my relationship with God. I was expecting a particular sound or method that I rarely received. I would become envious of others who would start a sentence with "The Lord said….." I did not have those experiences. My ego was injured and I often second guessed any unction or potential word that God gave me because I was unsure if it was really him speaking to me. I became a minister and I still had problems hearing from God. I did not know how to listen or what I was listening for.

A relationship without proper communication will not thrive. I could pray and read my bible, but I often failed at listening. I often failed at recognizing when it was actually God speaking to me versus my own voice wanting to do my own thing. Can you relate to this dilemma?

Over the course of time, I have learned that God communicates with his children in various ways. I was putting limits on my communication with the Lord by expecting him to speak in one specific way. The truth of the matter is that he has always been speaking to me in multiple ways....I just wasn't listening.

My journey on identifying God's voice has been a learning experience filled with highs and lows. In this book, I will share how I began to recognize God speaking to me in everyday lessons of life. I have learned (and still learning) how to identify opportunities to communicate with God. I have also learned that at times God is silent and that there is purpose in his silence. I invite you to continue reading so that you will not miss any more opportunities hearing God speak to you.

LaWanda C. Todd

Chapter 1 –

You Don't Have To Faint, But You Can If You Want To

I was sitting in church one day in the minister's corner during service. I had on the "face" that said I had it together. I wasn't feeling the greatest physically, but everyone already knew that. What they didn't know was I was sick spiritually. I was weary. I was despondent. I was spent. I was tired. I didn't know how much longer I could hold it together. I am not a cry baby, but I couldn't stop the tears from falling lately. I was overwhelmed because I didn't know what my purpose was, what I wanted to do with my life and why I couldn't keep my family and finances together. I was just tired of being the one always helping others, but couldn't help myself. Didn't have the time or energy to do it. I was tired of trying to come up with the answers and plans. Why can't they figure it out? I wasn't asking or expecting anyone to help me. I just wanted to be able to breathe and help myself. I went to church heavy. I knew I needed to make contact with my Heavenly Father. My heart was saying "I need some strength Lord….a touch…..some clarity….something…anything." The rest of me was on mute. The guest choir started singing "God is on my side" by the Mississippi Mass Choir. That is all I needed to hear. I knew that song was going to escort me into glory. It was just what I needed at that moment. As the choir continued to sing it, I started to feel the spirit touch my very soul. The words of the song began to minister to me; …"*Some days are weary and you can't see your way, some nights are lonely, with no one to say, you can make it, it's only a test, you can take it and don't you think nothing less, so wipe the tears from your eyes, God's on your side, hold on don't quit, God's on your side, HE can handle it, God's on your side…*" All I could say was "Thank you Lord for sending this choir to sing this song just for me." As I was responding to the song by entering into praise and worship, I felt someone tapping me. One of the sisters at the church was trying to get my attention. She had a condition that caused her to faint or pass out from time to time. We were familiar with this and knew what medication to give her when this occurred. She was shaking and I could tell she was about to pass out. She looked how I felt. She needed help. She collapsed in my arms. I held her and was able to get her into the seat. Everyone was caught up into the service and didn't really notice what was going on. I finally got one of the minister's attention to get me some water for her so my sister could take her medication. I didn't panic. I knew what to do. The choir continued to sing, but I couldn't enjoy it. I had to push the pause button for what I needed in order to tend to someone else's needs. My sister needed me and I HAD to be there for her. She slowly started to come around. I was able to give her the medication and water. She remained in my arms and was very weak. I looked up and mostly everyone else was on their feet being ministered to by the choir. Not many noticed us. I have to be honest, when I saw everyone else caught up in glory, I got jealous and upset. All I could think was I can't get what I need because here I go again, making sure someone else gets what they need. Understand, I was not upset with my sister. She could not help what was happening to her. Again, I was not upset with my sister, I was concerned for her. But in that moment, I was upset with myself. This episode was symbolic of what my life looked like lately. As the choir was finishing up the song, I was able to lean my sister against the chairs. I stood up and was able to praise the Lord for the remainder of the song. I did not receive from the Lord what I desperately needed that day. I was able to make sure that my sister got what she needed and she became well. I hoped that one day I could help myself the same way I had helped others.

Lesson: Days later, as I was still depleted, the Lord spoke to me in a still small voice. He replayed what happened at church and play by play he pointed out how my life, at that point, was synonymous with the incident that occurred. He showed me how this episode was an example of my life and the reason why I have been so burdened and didn't have much strength. I am the fixer. I am a professional at catering to and helping everyone else. Sadly, I do not apply that same professionalism to helping myself. I cut myself short by putting more focus on trying to fix everything for everyone else. I often don't give them an opportunity to go to God because I attempt to fix things for them when they come to me. I know I am a great friend, wife, daughter, mom...etc. Not perfect, but great. Everyone depends on, expects and knows I am going to fix it, do it, figure it out and make it happen. And I usually do. Not bragging, it is what it is....but 90% of the time, I am doing it in my own strength. I get burned out every time. When my sister at church reached out to me for help, I took my focus off of God and gave her what I had in me, which wasn't much because I was nearly on empty. I became resentful and frustrated, again not with her because I knew she couldn't help it. My frustration wasn't with her....it was with myself for not feeling like it was ok for me to put Wanda first. Now of course tending to my sister was important, but also remember, I knew I needed an encounter with God. I didn't know how to be selfish without guilt. I knew my sister was going to be ok. But I wasn't. I desperately wanted to be ok. I didn't want to miss my moment, so as the choir was coming to a close on the song, I just started saying Hallelujah. I had to get something in. I had to get a praise in. I needed to feel something in that moment. As I began to praise God, my sister started coming around and she sat up and was alert enough to take her 2nd dose of medication and drink water on her own. God took care of her, like he always does. I needed to allow him to take care of me.

The choir finished that song and we praised God as a church. I got a "little" touch from the Lord that helped me to see that there is so much more I need from him. I have to learn how to be ok with not catering to everyone else and cater to myself. I have to learn that not everyone's emergency is my emergency. That day, I needed God desperately and I still need him now. I have to go after him and lay aside everything that might be a distraction. This includes my loved ones that drain me sometimes because I let them. The moment I let my sister at church go and stood up, God took care of her. The lesson I learned was that instead of depleting myself trying to help everyone else, I need to let them go so that they can learn to lean on God for themselves. No, this doesn't mean that I cut off everyone and do not help when I can. What it does mean is that I will not try to fix life for them. I learned that I need to stop exhausting myself trying to be God. My intentions were good. My method was wrong. I gave out so much that I had nothing left to offer my savior. He allowed this moment to happen so I could see and hear him clearly. It is not easy letting go of that fixer mentality, but it can be done. Slowly but surely, I started to realize it was acceptable for me to take care of myself and dare I say, put myself first! When I say putting myself first, I simply mean placing me as a priority and realizing I am worth the same effort that I give others. Oftentimes, when you are a fixer or helper to others, rarely do you do the same for yourself. Due to neglect, low self-esteem or not realizing your worth. A lot of times taking care of others is a purposeful distraction because we don't want to deal with ourselves and our issues! How could I help anyone else when I could not help myself? I have learned and I am continuing to learn that I must feed my spirit before I attempt to feed others. I have also learned it is ok for me to say no to others so that I can say yes to God. When you get to the place where helping others is killing you, it is time to re-evaluate your methods and motives.

Scriptures:

1 Corinthians 6:19-20New King James Version (NKJV)

[19] Or do you not know that your body is the temple of the Holy Spirit who is in you, whom you have from God, and you are not your own? [20] For you were bought at a price; therefore glorify God in your body and in your spirit, which are God's.

> You are important. Take care of your temple.
> You cannot glorify God in a rundown temple.
> Invest in yourself.

1 Timothy 4:14-16New King James Version (NKJV)

[14] Do not neglect the gift that is in you, which was given to you by prophecy with the laying on of the hands of

the eldership. ¹⁵ Meditate on these things; give yourself entirely to them, that your progress may be evident to all. ¹⁶ Take heed to yourself and to the doctrine. Continue in them, for in doing this you will save both yourself and those who hear you.

Do not neglect your gifts and greatness. When you are at your best you will help yourself and those connected to you.

Mark 12:31New King James Version (NKJV)

³¹ And the second, like it, is this: 'You shall love your neighbor as yourself' There is no other commandment greater than these."

How can you validate or explain taking care of others better than you take care of yourself? The Love and care you show to others must begin at home...within you.

Consider this: Before an airplane leaves the runway, the flight attendant goes over the safety instructions. One of the main things the passengers are told to do is if there is a need for the oxygen masks to come down, put your own mask on first before you assist others with putting their masks on.

Interrogation Time: Ask yourself these tough questions. Be honest. Write your answers down and begin to pray for God to give you guidance on how to reverse being drained.

1.) What parts of your life cause the greatest frustration and exhaustion?

2.) Can this frustration and exhaustion be prevented? How?

3.) Have you considered that you are the reason that someone else is drained?

4.) Do you know how to set limits and say no?

_____
_____
_____
_____
_____
_____
_____
_____
_____
_____
_____
_____
_____
_____
_____
_____

Chapter 2:

Pressure, Pain and Puss Working Together

I got my right upper ear cartilage pierced for my 39th birthday in January. I know that might seem a tad bit old to be getting a piercing, but I just wanted to do something different on my last birthday before the big 40. I had my cartilage pierced before as a teenager and it was ok then. I eventually let it close up. After I got it pierced, I expected it to be sore for a while, but the soreness lasted longer than expected. I couldn't sleep on the right side of my body because it hurt to lay on that ear. This lasted for months. I cleaned it like I should've in the beginning. But I did slack off some. In April I changed the original piercing earring for a hoop. I figured that it was past time to change the earring. When my friend took out the original stud, it started bleeding. That was odd because it should have been healed by that time. It was painful but I endured it. I figured that changing the earring would help with the pain I was having and not being able to sleep on my right side. Changing the earring did help a little bit, but it was still sore. In May, my daughter Taryn said something to me about my ear. She asked me why it was white. I didn't pay her much attention and just kept doing what I was doing. I went to the bathroom and as I got out the shower I noticed white pus running down my ear. It was gross and I started freaking out. I called my husband, Terrence, to the bathroom…yes, I was still naked. I asked him to take the hoop out my ear. Blood and pus was running out of it. He tried to pull the earring out and he couldn't get it. The more he pulled on the earring, the louder I screamed and the more it hurt. It hurt so badly and I screamed so loud my daughter came from the other end of the house to see what was going on. She looked at my ear and said "I told you it was white! It is swollen and looks nasty." I guess I had an infection. My hubby finally got the earrings out but I still had an abscess on my ear filled with pus and blood. He tried to squeeze it out and I almost jumped onto the counter. It hurt so badly!!!! I told him to stop. I couldn't take the pain. Leave the abscess there. I was familiar with the pain from the piercing but this pain from the squeezing was worse and I could not handle it. He and my daughter said no. The abscess had to be squeezed so all the nastiness can be pushed out or else it would get worse. They are abscess, pimple and boil experts. I reluctantly agreed to allow them to perform a ghetto operation on my ear. My daughter held me down by wrapping her arms around me and my husband squeezed the abscess. The pain brought tears to my eyes. I hollered and screamed, screamed and hollered. I told him to stop again. Just leave it. I can't take anymore. He told me he almost got all of it…just another good squeeze and that should be all of it. I said no. I gave up. I couldn't do it. I was feeling weak and knew if I passed out, my family would not put a decent outfit on me when they called the ambulance to come get me. I could not continue with this process. It was entirely too painful. In my defiant temper tantrum I caught a glimpse of my nasty looking ear through my tears in the mirror. It looked like a crime scene. I was so caught up in feeling the pain that I did not actually see what was occurring. I could not believe so much nastiness and junk came from that little piercing. I knew I couldn't let my ear stay in the shape it was. I had to man up and let hubby finish what he was doing. I grabbed the counter, my daughter held me and I let him squeeze the rest of the blood and pus out of it. I screamed and cried. After I couldn't take it no more for real this time, he stopped and said he got it all. My ear was sore, it looked ugly, but the original pain was gone. The pain I had in my ear since January, the past 5 months was gone. He put Band-Aids and ointment on my ear. My family laughed at me and I was a little warm with them for laughing but I felt better. I took those earrings and threw them in the garbage. I went to bed that night and for the 1st time in 5 months, I was able to sleep on right side. When I woke up that morning and took bandages off, the swelling was gone and you could hardly tell that I had an issue with that ear. There was a small scar, but that's all. Within a few days, you couldn't see a thing. You cannot tell it was even pierced.

Lesson: The Lord laid it on my heart to share this experience as a testimony at a church service to bless someone else. At the time, I did not have the "Lesson" yet. I did not know what was going to come out of my mouth. The Lord caught me on a good day and I shared my experience. As I was sharing it, he gave me what to say in that very hour as the lesson. There is a painful situation going on in your life. A situation that has lingered longer than it should have. Part of your calling requires you to go through a process. That process is painful at times. You may have stumbled into it, you may have put your hands in God's business, you may have simply been ordained to go through this period in your life so that God can get some glory. But you cannot stop the process. You may be naked and exposed. No longer able to cover up what is broken. It is painful, but you got to go through it. You cannot keep stopping and starting. You cannot keep asking God for deliverance and then when he brings it, you tell him "Not that way Lord." You are almost there to the finish line. Don't you dare give up. Don't you dare give in!!! Let him process you. Let him squeeze the junk out. Let him use your pain for his glory. Doesn't matter who is laughing at you or what they are saying. Let the process be complete. Let him finish the work. When he does, you will barely have a scar, but you will have the memory of what God can and will do for you. You will be better after the process. You will be stronger and wiser. But you got to go through it. Let him push the infection out. Let him push the mess out. Just as my Husband was pushing the puss out and my daughter was holding me, God is pushing out what is unfruitful and poison in your life and the Holy Spirit is wrapping his arms around you for comfort. At that time, the word was for someone else. I have since embraced it as a word for me too. Nothing happens without God's permission. If a painful process is occurring allow God carry you through every step. Resistance will only delay your deliverance.

Scriptures:

Psalm 27:14New King James Version (NKJV)

14 Wait on the LORD; be of good courage, And He shall strengthen your heart; Wait, I say, on the LORD!

> Don't give up. Decide to be strong. He is carrying you through the process and gives you strength daily. Wait for the process to be complete and you will reap his benefits.

Hosea 6:1-2New King James Version (NKJV)

Come, and let us return to the LORD; For He has torn, but He will heal us; He has stricken, but He will bind us up.² After two days He will revive us; On the third day He will raise us up, That we may live in His sight.

> Whatever the Lord is tearing down, trust and believe he will rebuild, even better than it originally was! We cannot live in his sight full of puss and mess.

Zechariah 13:9New King James Version (NKJV)

⁹ I will bring the one–third through the fire, Will refine them as silver is refined, And test them as gold is tested. They will call on My name, And I will answer them. I will say, 'This is My people'; And each one will say, 'The LORD is my God.'

> The process requires us to be tested through the fire. God sees you. He is claiming you. He will answer you.

Consider this: A woman in labor cannot stop the birthing process once the baby has started to descend. There are things that can be done to delay the birth, but it cannot be stopped. Studies show that women who are calm and present during the labor process have much better results, less injuries, quicker deliveries and recoveries versus women that are difficult and put up a fight against the process.

Interrogation Time: Ask yourself these tough questions. Be honest. Write your answers down and begin to pray for God to give you the strength to endure the pressure, pain and puss you are experiencing or have to experience in order to be free.

1.) What is inside of you that you feel needs to come out or that you know you need to be delivered from?

2.) Are you in the midst of a struggle with God over a certain process? Why?

3.) Have you stopped your process and as a result you are not whole or injured?

4.) Are you willing to remain in the fire for his glory?

_____

_____

_____

_____

_____

_____

_____

_____

_____

_____

_____

_____

_____

_____

_____

_____

_____

_____

_____

_____

_____

_____

Chapter 3:

Do You See What I See?

Elijah and I were riding in the car. He was in the booster seat. He had to be about 4 years old. As we were traveling, I saw something flying around in the car. Initially thinking it was a fly or another small irritating insect I just brushed it off. As it started flying closer to me and more in my face, I realized it was a wasp. It was huge (to me anyway). Just like most females, I do not like bugs. They are not one of my favorite creations. Upon realizing that I had a wasp in my car, I starting screaming and wailing my hands to get it out of my face. I managed to roll down the windows, but it would not fly out. I continued to drive, scream and act a fool because I could see the wasp and knew that it could sting me and I did not want that to happen. Obviously my eyes were not totally on the road nor was I able to focus on my drive or destination because this wasp had me jacked up. I do not even remember where we going. I just knew this wasp had me consumed in that moment. The wasp flew into the back seat near Elijah. Ok, I will be honest since you pulled it out of me. I was ever so grateful that the wasp was in the back with Elijah. If he got stung, I could comfort him, get him a Happy Meal with a toy and he would be ok. If it stung me, I might die. Ok, maybe not die, but it would not be enjoyable. I was just glad it was out of my face even though it was still lingering. Elijah was calm and looked at me (I could see him through the rearview mirror) and said "Why are you scared and screaming? It's just a butterfly!!!" Elijah looked at the wasp, did not act crazy like I did and remained calm. He was fearless. Eventually, the wasp flew out the window. Elijah had no idea how his 4 year old words would impact me.

Lesson: God spoke to me through 4 year old Elijah. I was panicking over so many things, reacting in unbelief. I was worried, scared and frustrated. Situations were before me and I felt overwhelmed. I was looking at my mountains and was using all of my strength to move them. I was getting all worked up. I wasn't looking at God. I was looking at me. When Elijah said it's "only a butterfly", God was saying "Wanda, stop overreacting in your flesh. Look at the situation through spiritual eyes." Butterflies are beautiful, harmless creatures. They emerge from a slightly disgusting process and another insect, the caterpillar. Butterflies are the product of a process. Butterflies can't hurt you because every hurtful thing has already been squeezed out of them. I know many people that are afraid of bugs and insects. I do not know anyone that is afraid of butterflies. Instead of getting scared and doubtful of situations in our lives because we see the "wasp" and we know the sting, we need to see the "butterfly" in the situation and the beauty in it. Instead of having a wasp reaction, we need to have a butterfly reaction. A butterfly reaction is one of faith and confidence knowing that nothing by any means shall hurt you. A butterfly reaction is a soul assured that God is in control. Everything will be ok because God's got you. There have been countless times in my life that I allowed my flesh to flare up in worry, doubt, unbelief, anxiety, fear and depression because all I could see was the mountains and impossibilities. All I could see were the wasps. I feared the sting. I had uncountable sleepless nights. I have stressed myself to the point of being physically sick from worry. I blocked the peace of God. My mind was cluttered with wasp fear. God used a 4 year old to get my attention. God used a 4 year old to make me examine myself and my relationship with God. I had more faith in the enemy than I did in God. How? Because I was reacting off of what the devil presented before me and what he was doing. I believed he was going to complete his assignment. I believed he would win. I believed what I saw. I gave into my emotions. I gave into hopelessness. I gave into panic and worry. God did not want me to be overwhelmed with the situation. He wanted me to see the beauty in it which was him being with me the entire way. He wanted me to see him as big and my problems as small. He wanted me to see his glory and his power. He was in control even though it appeared he was nowhere to be found. He wanted me to make the choice; to see the butterfly instead of the wasp. He wanted me to choose peace over chaos. He wanted me to choose faith over doubt. He wanted me to see the situation through eyes of faith and trust and not through fear and anxiety. Thank you Lord for showing me the butterfly in every situation.

Scriptures:

Isaiah 26:3New King James Version (NKJV)

³ You will keep him in perfect peace, Whose mind is stayed on You, Because he trusts in You.

> Don't allow you mind to waver between faith and doubt. Get focused and stay focused.

Luke 10:19New King James Version (NKJV)

¹⁹ Behold, I give you the authority to trample on serpents and scorpions, and over all the power of the enemy, and nothing shall by any means hurt you

> You got the power! Use it!

Romans 8:28New King James Version (NKJV)

²⁸ And we know that all things work together for good to those who love God, to those who are the called according to His purpose.

> It will work out for you according to his will. Stop trippin!

Isaiah 54:17New King James Version (NKJV)

[17] No weapon formed against you shall prosper, And every tongue which rises against you in judgment You shall condemn. This is the heritage of the servants of the LORD, And their righteousness is from Me," Says the LORD.

> Remember who has got your back. Remember who you belong to!

Consider this: Wearing glasses is supposed to enhance or correct problem vision. Wearing the wrong prescription glasses can create more of a problem. Is it advised to have your vision checked regularly. When was your last spiritual eye exam?

Interrogation Time: Ask yourself these tough questions. Be honest. Write your answers down and begin to pray for God to correct your faulty vision.

1.) Are you experiencing anxiety or depression over what you see in your situation?

2.) Are you focused on the mountain in your way?

3.) Are you being a drama queen or king because you do not like what you are seeing? Have you considered changing your perception?

Chapter 4:

Just Dive In!

Elijah loves the water. He loves taking showers and baths. He loves going to the beach. He was a 6 year old fish. He didn't know how to swim, but he loved playing in the water. He stays in bath tubs until the water is cold. One hot summer day, I took him to my friend's house that had a swimming pool. I had planned for us to have a nice summer day in the backyard pool. I didn't really know how to swim either and had a fear of the water, but I was fine with this pool because I could stand up in it. It was 18 ft. around and 4 and ½ feet tall. I was going to be the big kid, the only adult, in a pool full of kids. We got to my friend's house. I put a floatable vest on Elijah. He had his Teenage mutant ninja turtle swim trunks on. He was ready to go.

A few of the kids were already in the pool as Elijah climbed up the stairs. There were also kids behind him. When Elijah got to the top of the steps, he looked in the pool and had a change of heart. He immediately got scared and did not want to get in the water. He started panicking and made everyone that was on the steps climb back down so he could get off the ladder and back on the ground. I don't think I have ever seen him so afraid. I tried to talk to him to get back on the ladder and into the pool but at that moment, he didn't want to do it. Others in the pool tried to convince him to get in the pool and he still said no. The rest of us got in the pool and left him on the outside. Everyone was having fun. I guess Elijah got jealous and wanted to get in on the fun. He slowly made his way back onto the stairs and everyone was rooting for him to get into the pool. He got to the top of the stairs and got frightened again. He started to go back down the stairs, but Taryn picked him up and put him on a floatation device. He was finally in the pool, but still terrified. Someone had to be holding onto the floaty the entire time he was on it. He was not relaxed at all. If he thought someone was going to let go, he started hyperventilating and crying. No one else that was holding the floaty could have any fun because they were too busy catering to him to enjoy themselves. After about 2 hours of trying to coax Eli to get into the pool and have some fun, I got tired. I went in the house to change my clothes. Slowly but surely, all the other kids in the pool started coming in the house and changing their clothes. After a while, I noticed that all the kids had been accounted for…except Elijah. I looked all over the house for him and couldn't find him. I had no idea where he could have been. I started asking the other kids and no one knew where he was at. Finally, someone said "Oh, Eli is still in the pool". I panicked. My heart zipped open my chest and jumped out on the ground and just laid there. I ran outside. Why would they leave him alone knowing he couldn't swim and was afraid?!?!?! I thought the worse…but when I got to the pool, I could not believe what I was seeing. Elijah was playing in the water, he was "swimming", and he was jumping, laughing, having a ball, OFF the floaty, and doing all sorts of things in the water. When he saw me, he said "I'm not scared anymore". He had spent the last 2 hours frightened to death. He spent the last 2 hours wrestling with his fears. He spent the last 2 hours missing out on the things that everyone else was enjoying. He spent the last 2 hours holding up a few others fun because he was going back and forth with getting in and out the pool. Finally, the last 5 minutes of time we had left, he decided that he was going to take the plunge and go for it. It was great that he did that, but look at the 2 hours that he missed by allowing fear to hold him hostage.

Lesson: A while later, when I was going through a trial, The Lord brought this back to my remembrance. I was Elijah. God had called me to do so many things over the years. I would start out to do them, but wouldn't complete it. I would see what was required of me and I would go back down the ladder. There was a particular situation that God was calling me to go higher in. After giving every excuse I had in me not to do it, God let me know that I didn't have a choice but to do his will. I girded myself up. I pumped myself up. I encouraged myself to do what God had asked me to do. I stepped out on the ladder to do it, but when I saw the weight of glory, I went back down the stairs. Fear had me paralyzed in my mind. Fear had me in a place of torment. Fear had me more afraid of it than God. I can't even tell you what I was really fearful of….maybe failing, maybe succeeding, maybe of what I knew I was going to lose…or gain. Whatever it was, it kept me paralyzed longer than I can remember. The Lord showed me areas of my life that mimicked what Elijah had done. One particular part that he let me see clear as day was when Elijah decided not to get into the pool and he made everyone else get off the ladder behind him so he could climb back down. He held them up and delayed their fun. He delayed their blessing. The Lord let me know that I was holding up his blessings over my family. They were right behind me on the ladder, but every time I backed down, they had to back down too. They couldn't get their blessings because I was holding them up with my disobedience. When I finally faced my fear, I got on the ladder thinking that once I got to the top, I would have the safety and security of a floaty to help me ease my way into the deep. My floaty was the help and support of others. My floaty was the safety net of my family and friends. My floaty was the comfort of my Pastors and church family. But the Lord let me know, I was not going to have a floaty as I have had before. He wanted me to launch out into the deep and HE would be my floaty. He knew if I had any floaty other than him, I would hold onto it forever. I would keep floating, but never get around to swimming. Once I understood what the Lord was saying to me, I got myself together. I got rid of the excuses. Climbed the ladder. Didn't look for a floaty and just launched out into the deep. I dove in. The fear was still there, but I dove in anyway. God blessed. He always does. I wish I had done it sooner.

Scriptures:

2 Timothy 1:7New King James Version (NKJV)

⁷ For God has not given us a spirit of fear, but of power and of love and of a sound mind.

> You have everything you need already inside of you. Don't be intimidated by the enemy.

1 John 4:18New King James Version (NKJV)

¹⁸ There is no fear in love; but perfect love casts out fear, because fear involves torment. But he who fears has not been made perfect in love.

> Fear will torment you more than people will if you allow it.

Revelation 21:8New King James Version (NKJV)

⁸ But the cowardly, unbelieving, abominable, murderers, sexually immoral, sorcerers, idolaters, and all liars shall have their part in the lake which burns with fire and brimstone, which is the second death."

Being a coward (fearful) will not only cause you to miss out on the blessings of God, but can also guarantee a spot for you in hell. Fear is a real emotion, but don't allow it to keep you from doing the will of God.

Hebrews 13:5New King James Version (NKJV)

[5] *Let your* conduct *be* without covetousness; *be* content with such things as you have. For He Himself has said, "I will never leave you nor forsake you."

He isn't going anywhere. God's got you!

Consider This: Dorothy, The Scarecrow, The Lion and The Tin man had everything that they needed already inside of them. Their journey to see the Wizard helped them to discover it. The wicked witch and every other distraction pushed them further along their journey and helped to identify their strengths.

Interrogation Time: Ask yourself these tough questions. Be honest. Write your answers down and begin to pray for God to help you identify your fears and how to move past them.

1.) How many years has fear held you hostage?

2.) Is the thing that you fear really that bad?

3.) How did face and overcome other fears that you have had in your life?

4.) Are you more afraid of what people will say or think instead of being obedient to God?

_____

_____

_____

_____

_____

_____

_____

_____

_____

_____

_____

_____

_____

_____

_____

_____

_____

_____

_____

_____

_____

_____

_____

Chapter 5:
I Will Start Again...AGAIN!!!

I have tried countless times to lose weight. I have tried diets, exercise plans, personal trainers, various gym memberships, pills, drinks, contraptions…etc. If it has been created, I have probably tried it in some form. The reason why I have tried so many different forms of diet and exercise is because most didn't work how I wanted them to work. I would try one method. When I wouldn't get the results I wanted, I would stop that particular plan. I would talk bad about the plan because it didn't work….or maybe I didn't know how to work it. Either way, after a time doing the plan with little or no results I was done. I gave up. I didn't look back. I counted it as a loss and failure. I would move on to the next trick or plan. That was my vicious dieting cycle for more than 20 years. If I did lose a pound or two, by the time I gave up on that particular plan, I would gain more than I lost. On one of my dieting and exercise "adventures" I started off pretty good with following the plan. I lost weight in the 1st week. I was excited. I figured this must be the plan for me. I lost a few pounds the 2nd week. Hot dang! This was the plan for me…until the 3rd week….I lost nothing. Week 4, the scale moved up a couple of pounds. Week 5, still no change. Here we go again. Nothing ever works for me. I got frustrated and tired of things not working out for me. I give my all and do what I'm supposed to do but nothing ever works out for me. I give up. I will just be beautifully chunky forever. This is just too much work. I had given up on yet another plan because it didn't yield the results that I thought it should. Granted, my plan warned that stalls or plateaus may occur, but I didn't think it would happen to me. I started asking other people about their results. Some were not very encouraging. My "failure" seemed worse after talking with them. I tried not to think about being stuck and not seeing any results. It was hard. I finally got to the point of after several weeks of not seeing results that I gave up. I didn't even want to move on to the next best things. I just gave up and became hopeless. Several weeks into this process, I still wasn't seeing a loss on the scale. One morning, I got on the scale. I did this every morning as it was my habit. When I got on the scale, I had lost 2lbs. I couldn't believe my eyes. I wanted to make sure the scale wasn't broke, so I stepped off and got back up there again. Once again the scale said that I had lost 2lbs. I think I jumped up and clicked my heels. The next day I weighed, I lost another pound. I was super excited. By the end of the week I had lost 5lbs. I almost gave up on a plan that was working for me because I didn't see the immediate results. I later learned that my body was making adjustments that would not show up on the scale right away. I was measuring my success based off of what I saw. I was measuring my lack of success and presumed failure based off of others guidelines.

Lesson: Many times in our walk with God we commit and re-commit to do better. To trust God more. To have more faith. To read our bibles consistently. To prayer more often. To be faithful in paying our tithes. We come up with so many things to become spiritually fit just as I was trying to become physically fit. Each time I tried these things for my spiritual man, I started off great. I was excited to commit and do what I needed to do for my relationship with God. I knew I needed to be spiritually healthy. I would make my best attempts. When I got past the point of the plateau in the plan that I was talking about earlier, the Lord spoke to me and let me know that many times I have run out of patience and given up in my spiritual life. I didn't see immediately results and figured something was wrong. I was doing the right things, but I was impatient. I was looking through my natural eyes and not the eyes of faith. Countless times I have vowed to do better in my walk with the Lord by recommitting myself to do what I know is right to do. Countless times I have given up, let go of my commitment, lost hope, lost patience, lost my desire because I did not see immediate results or the results that I was hoping for. Again, I was looking through my natural eye. I did not see what was going on in the spirit. When I went over 1 month without losing weight, I was extremely focused on the scale. I was almost obsessed with it. It was torment each day, sometimes twice a day not to see the scale move. If I weighed in the morning, I was ill and had an attitude the rest of the day because I didn't have the result I wanted. During my weight loss journey I had started taking my measurements. At the end of the month when the scale did not move, I took my measurements. When I measured myself, I had lost 8 inches!!! I couldn't believe it. I started thinking and remembered a brand new skirt and pants that I had only worn once were now too big. In retrospect, even though the scale didn't move, I was still succeeding. I lost inches and went down a size. I was so focused on the indicator (the scale) that I hadn't noticed the actual result. The Lord let me know that even though I don't see the results in one area, he is interceding on my behalf in the spirit realm. There are things that I will never see until it's time for it to manifest. I was so focused on one thing, that I missed seeing the big picture. I was making progress, I just didn't see it. Patience was having her perfect work….and then I stopped it. I was almost to the point of giving up like I had done so many times in the past. This is the scheme of the devil. He wants us to lose faith. He knows that without faith it is impossible to please God. The Lord wants us to trust him even when we can't see him working. Don't stop praying for that child even though they seem to be getting worse. Don't stop paying your tithes and giving your offering even though you don't see the window of heaven open. Don't stop coming to church even though your situation hasn't changed. Don't stop speaking God's word even though it feels like nothing is changing. Trust and believe that behind the scenes Jesus Christ is working and moving on your behalf. Be diligent. Be faithful. Be consistent. Stick with the plan laid out in the word of God. Don't give up. Don't quit. Results will come.

Scripture:

Philippians 1:6New King James Version (NKJV)

⁶ being confident of this very thing that He who has begun a good work in you will complete it until the day of Jesus Christ;

> He is completing what he started in you whether you realize it or not.

Hebrews 6:12New King James Version (NKJV)

¹² that you do not become sluggish, but imitate those who through faith and patience inherit the promises.

> Giving up aborts the promises of God. Hang in there. Help isn't on the way, it is already there!

Hebrews 12:1New King James Version (NKJV)

12 Therefore we also, since we are surrounded by so great a cloud of witnesses, let us lay aside every

weight, and the sin which so easily ensnares us, and let
us run with endurance the race that is set before us,

This walk with Christ is not a sprint, but a marathon. Pace yourself.

Consider this: Even though the Hare should have beaten the Tortoise in the race, he didn't. Not because he wasn't capable, but because he underestimated the power of consistency and patience.

Interrogation Time: Ask yourself these tough questions. Be honest. Write your answers down and begin to pray for God to help you learn how to be consistent and to patiently endure the changes and improvements in your life.

1.) Why am I inconsistent? Why can't I keep my vows or promises to God?

2.) How often do I overlook results and answers to my prayers?

3.) What is the purpose of my relationship with God? Are we both benefitting from this relationship?

_____
_____
_____
_____

Chapter 6:

Is Your Thinking Getting In The Way?

Terrence and I were at an outdoor shopping outlet enjoying a beautiful day. The weather was perfect. We didn't have the kids with us. We weren't rushed for time. We were able to spend some quality time together. As we were walking down the strip, I could see in the distance a man sitting on a bench with his dog sitting on the ground in front of him. I am not a fan of animals at all. I immediately got apprehensive about having to walk in front of that dog. The dog looked like Lassie. I know that sounds all cute and cuddly, but I still didn't like the fact that I had to go near it. Why would this man bring a dog to a shopping outlet? The dog did not appear to be a service animal. As we got closer, I started thinking: "if this dog jumps on me, he will die." "If I walk past this dog and there is a pile of crap on the ground next to him, I'm going off!" "This man does not look the cleanest and the dog is probably dirtier than he looks!" I was having a full conversation in my head about this potentially wolf like, worm and flea infested creature that would not like me and would immediately pounce on me as soon as I walked past him. Yes, in my mind, this dog was the enemy. Yes, he would harm me. Yes, I had to continue to proceed with caution. Yes, I had to be willing to protect myself and take matters into my own hands if the dog came at me and I felt unsafe. I had my plan in place. Terrence was walking on the side closest to the dog, but the dog wouldn't go for him. He was only going to harm me. So I prepared myself to stomp and kick the dog when he came towards me. I was not going to run because I had my cute boots on and would not have gotten very far. Ok, I was ready to approach the dog now. We got to the bench and I proceeded with caution walking past the man and the dog. I eyed the dog down and let it know by my mean mug that I was not the one and today was not the day! The dog never flinched or moved. The dog didn't even look at me. We got passed the man and the dog without any issues. Thank God!

We went into a store as soon as we passed the man and the dog. We stayed in there for a few minutes. When we finally came out of the store, I couldn't help but notice a little boy that had to be 2 years old was running towards the dog. Yes, running to the dog! His parents were closely behind him but they could not stop the boy from getting to the dog before they did. The little boy reached the dog and immediately started hugging the dog! He was all over that dog. He had no inhibitions. He talked to the dog, hugged him, loved on him and the dog never resisted. T and I stopped for a second to see what was going on. The boy's parents thanked the man for allowing their son to interact with the dog, telling the man that their son loves dogs. My initial reaction was how in the world could those parents let their son hug on a strange dog that probably was worm and flea infested with possible Cujo-like tendencies!!! What if that dog bit their son? Who were they going to blame? What if that old man was a pedophile and was secretly getting turned on by watching the boy hug his dog? Those were my 1st thoughts, but my 2nd thoughts were that it was kind of cute to see the boy and dog hug. It wouldn't have been cute if it was me hugging the dog, but it was cute for someone else to be doing it. We turned away and continued to enjoy our beautiful day together.

Lesson: The Lord let me know that my thinking was distorted. This wasn't the 1st time. A lot of times our thinking gets in the way of what the Lord is trying to do. I had perceived all of these bad things about that dog. I didn't even give the dog a chance. I have actually only had one bad experience with a dog, but that experience has warped my thinking to the point that no dog stands a chance with me. There are times that Jesus wants us to just come to him. He doesn't want us to be apprehensive. He doesn't even want us to question him. He just wants us to come. He just wants us to trust. Just as the 2 year old boy ran up to that dog and hugged him, the Lord wants us to do the same thing. A lot of the time, we talk ourselves out of being intimate with the Lord. We allow the flesh to dictate 101 reasons why running to the Lord will not work. We allow common sense and what we see with our natural eye to dictate what will be. God doesn't work with common sense or eyes of flesh. He doesn't even address those things. The bible talks about us coming to the Lord or only being able to enter the kingdom like a child…this means that we trust God easily, does what he says without question. We don't allow our flesh and our minds lead us….we let our hearts lead. That little boy showed me that there were many time I walked past the Lord in a hurry rather than running to him with open arms and embracing whatever it is he has for me. My agenda items had priority. My schedule and to do list had to be completed first. This was my thought pattern. Then I began to think back on all the times of intimacy with my heavenly father I have missed out on because I thought or talked myself out of it. He would never hurt me and he always wants to love on me and wants me to love on him.

Scripture:

Isaiah 55:8, 9 New King James Version (NKJV)

[8] "For My thoughts are not your thoughts, Nor are your ways My ways," says the LORD. "For as the heavens are higher than the earth, So are My ways higher than your ways, And My thoughts than your thoughts.

We don't have all the answers. Stop thinking that you do.

Luke 11:17New King James Version (NKJV)

17 But He, knowing their thoughts, said to them: "Every kingdom divided against itself is brought to desolation, and a house divided against a house falls.

God's thoughts don't have to line up with yours. Your thoughts need to line up with his will. If they don't your relationship with his is divided.

Jeremiah 29:11New King James Version (NKJV)

11 For I know the thoughts that I think toward you, says the LORD, thoughts of peace and not of evil, to give you a future and a hope.

Stop over thinking. God has good things planned for you. Trust his plan.

Consider this: "Tell the negative committee that meets inside your head to sit down and shut up." – Ann Bradford.

Interrogation Time: Ask yourself these tough questions. Be honest. Write your answers down and begin to pray for God to help you restructure your thought life.

1.) How have your thoughts interfered with God's plan?

2.) How has your thoughts shaped you into the person you have become?

3.) In what ways have your thoughts taken over your life?

4.) Have you attempted to change your thought life before? How did this work for you?

_____

_____

_____

_____

_____

_____

_____

_____

_____

_____

_____

_____

_____

_____

_____

_____

_____

_____

_____

_____

_____

Chapter 7:

Control Issues

I hate doing laundry. Hate might be a strong word. I strongly dislike doing laundry. I don't like separating clothes, folding them and most of all, I very much strongly dislike putting the clothes away. I will leave them on the couch or in the basket and take out what I need when I need it before putting them away. That just makes more sense to me. Earlier in my marriage, I did the laundry most of the time. I just took it on as one of my wifely and motherly duties. I'm supposed to be superwoman and do it all right? From time to time my Husband would help with the laundry. Bless his heart, he tried. I remembered one time after I had given birth to my daughter, I came downstairs and saw piles of laundry on the couch. He had brought our nieces over to help out while I was recovering from my C-section. When I saw the clothes on the couch, I burst into tears (postpartum emotional wreck) and went back upstairs. Years later, I still had issues with my husband doing the laundry. He would sort the clothes but sometimes wouldn't wash things according to instructions, which left me with some discolored and shrunken clothes. He would also confuse my clothes with my daughter's clothes. I would be missing clothes and then see my daughter wearing them. Now she knew they were not hers, but she didn't take responsibility for that. She would say they were put in her pile. She would blame her dad. His excuse was he didn't know. Moments like that caused me not to appreciate or really want his help with the laundry. We have always heard and said, if you want something done right, do it yourself. In his attempts to help me, as I allowed him, the thing that irked me the absolute most was the way that he folded up the towels. I had a system of how I wanted MY towels folded. I wanted them to all look the same way in the cabinet and fit a certain way. I felt it was best that they were folded the short way to accommodate the space they were going in. My husband just folded them….no rhyme or reason or purpose……he just folded them. Annnnnnddddddd he didn't do it the same way each time! I tried to show him the correct way, MY way, on how to fold the towels. My way of showing him was unfolding each towel he had taken the time to fold, looking at him with disgust, and then proceeded to fold the towels MY way. He got the hint after several of these unfolding episodes, but he still did it his way. The way that worked for him. Now, I know someone is saying, at least he is helping you and I was somewhat grateful. The bigger issue was that he wasn't doing it the way I wanted him to do it and therefore I didn't consider it help, especially if I had to go back and redo it my way, the right way. Life goes on and I continued my attempts to be supermom and wife but severe burnout was approaching. It was just too much to try to do everything. After a series of different events, I hit a brick wall. I was completely burnt out. As women, we sometimes keep the motor running. Never stopping to refuel, get an oil change or inspection. We just keep going until the wheels fall off.

Very rarely do we ask for what we need. Sometimes we don't even know what it is that we need. I confessed to my husband that I was burnt out and needed help with the kids and around the house because I was becoming bitter and resentful. After some discussions and other events that occurred in our life, my husband had taken on a different role in our home. My husband has not officially been diagnosed as having Obsessive Compulsive Disorder, but anyone who knows him will agree that he has undiagnosed OCD. Everything has to be in its place and everything has to be in order at all times. If it's not, it drives him crazy. Which in turn drives me, Tay, Taryn and Eli crazy. Think of the TV show "Monk" if the character was played by a black man, my husband would get the part without even auditioning. He took over the housecleaning duties in the house. That was such a weight lifted off of me. He is an amazing housekeeper. Better than me by a long shot. Now of course we do things differently, but hey, as long as the dishes get cleaned, does it really matter if runs the water while washing them or plugs the sink up to eliminate running water? One of the things he started specializing in was doing the laundry. He would wash our clothes almost daily. He would make sure the sheets and comforters and pillows were washed weekly. He was walking in his anointing. I would come home from a long day of work and he would have the clothes washed, dried and folded and I would just have to put mine away. His towel game was still off in my eyes, but I let that slide. After months of this new dynamic in my home, one day I went to the towel cabinet and noticed that all of the towels were facing the same way and folded the same way. I knew I hadn't folded any of them, but miraculously…they were all uniformed and that made me extremely happy. Now, I cannot tell you when the change occurred. I cannot tell you if the light bulb finally went off in my husband head and he learned to fold towels my way. I cannot tell you if he even changed his way of folding towels. Maybe I changed how I looked at the towels. Maybe I considered his way was better than my way. The part of when the change occurred I really cannot pinpoint. But I am forever grateful that I hardly ever have to fold towels anymore.

Lesson: I was driving down the street one day and the Lord reminded me a lot of things that I get worked up over is my fault. In my mind, things should be done a certain way and at a certain time. Those things make sense to me. They may even be great ideas and thoughts. The Lord spoke to me and reminded me that his ways aren't my ways. I had "suffered" with the affliction of laundry for many years. I had dreaded it, but did it because I knew it needed to be done. I didn't accept or receive the help that I wanted because it wasn't done in the way I felt it should have been done. So I suffered through it. The Lord let me know, he has always been there to prevent me from being burnt out in the first place. I kept going to him after the burn out occurred instead of allowing him to help me in the beginning. I would do things my way. I had plenty of great intentions but I was doing those things in my own strength and not being led of God. I often had seeds of bitterness in my heart because I was doing good things with the wrong motive or doing things I didn't need to be doing in the first place. I had to be in control and it had to be done my way! The Lord let me know that I was making things harder than they needed to be simply because I would not seek him first. I was suffering through and with things that he never meant for me to suffer with. I would ask the Lord for help....but I wanted him to help me in the way I thought was best. If the Lord answered me or offered help to me the same way my husband was folding towels, I let the Lord know in my own way, that I didn't like how he was helping me. For example, I asked the Lord to help me deal with someone on my job that was a trouble maker. Now, when I asked the Lord to fire that person or transfer them to another department. The person got a promotion and raise! I was like Lord.....this isn't helping me. Never mind Lord, I will just fill out applications and find another job. Another example is when I asked God to help me with lower back pain that I was having for a while. I wanted God to take the pain away. He didn't. Instead, I had to manage my pain with medication, steroid injections and physical therapy. Lord, why are you not helping me how I want you to help me and why aren't you doing it MY way???? When my prayers weren't answered my way or to my satisfaction, I just did what I thought was best. Again, if you want something done right, do it yourself. I had even gotten to the point of not even asking the Lord for certain things because I knew or assumed he wouldn't answer how I wanted him too. No, I wasn't smoking or sniffing anything. Our savior is such a gentleman that he never forced his ways on me. He just stood back and let me be foolish for a while until I came to him, burnt out to a crisp, and finally ready to let go of my way of doing things in exchange for his ways. I felt like an idiot. I was bringing unnecessary stress and issues on myself because I wouldn't let go of my ways. Father, forgive me. That day the Lord revealed this to me made me realize the blessings of peace that I missed because I wouldn't let go of my controlling ways. My husband has always been able to do laundry. I just didn't allow him to do it his way. I missed years of laundry deliverance because I would not let go of having complete control. I can proudly say today that I am delivered from that laundry demon. I don't dread it when I have to do it. I follow my husband's lead with the laundry. He does the majority of the work with it and whatever he asks me to do to help him I do it. By following his lead and letting go of my way of doing it, I get to enjoy the benefits. I have clean underwear and socks all the time. My clothes have that wonderful Gain scent to them. I sleep on fresh out the dryer sheets and comforters. I don't have to separate whites and darks, I don't have to wonder the origin of stains from the kid's clothes. When our dryer decided to give up the ghost, I did not have to tote any clothes to and from the laundry mat. My husband does it all. Is that not a blessing! It's the same with the Lord, we miss out because we won't give him the reigns. Your issue may be much more serious than laundry, but the lesson is the same. We are losing control buy trying to keep control. Allow the expert, our Savior, to do what he does. If he needs your help, he will ask for it. He has been around much longer than all of us. He is certified and experienced in his field. His resume is impeccable. He is recognized around the universe. He has never made a mistake or lost a case. He is the great "I AM". Whatever you need him to be in moments of your life, allow him to be it. He knows what he is doing. I recommend that you consult him on the front end instead of the back end. You can avoid many things and sustain his peace if you let him do his job.

Scriptures:

Matthew 11:28-30New King James Version (NKJV)

28 Come to Me, all you who labor and are heavy laden, and I will give you rest. 29 Take My yoke upon you and learn from Me, for I am gentle and lowly in heart, and you will find rest for your souls. 30 For My yoke is easy and My burden is light."

Do you like carrying that heavy burden? You don't have to!

James 1:6-8New King James Version (NKJV)

6 But let him ask in faith, with no doubting, for he who doubts is like a wave of the sea driven and tossed by *the wind. ⁷ For let not that man suppose that he will receive anything from the Lord; ⁸ he is a double-minded man, unstable in all his ways.*

Trying to retain control shows lack of faith in God. God responds to faith and trust in him, not to faith and trust in yourself.

Consider this: Pursuing to be the person that is always right, may cause you to get left.

Interrogation Time: Ask yourself these tough questions. Be honest. Write your answers down and begin to pray for God to help you to relinquish control of your life over to him.

1.) How have your control issues blocked blessings in your life?

2.) Why is it necessary for you to retain control?

3.) Why is it so hard for you to trust God with total control over your life?

_____

_____

_____

_____

_____

_____

_____

Chapter 8:

Stop Playing With My Emotions!

We were having a revival at church with a guest prophet. Many of us love when a prophet comes and gives us a word. We are usually hoping to hear confirmation of prosperity, new husband, house, car or something good along those lines. Towards the end of the service, the prophet came to me and said "God says you owe him another child." That was all she said. Now this left me quite puzzled. My husband and I didn't really have a conversation about having more kids. We were content with Tay and Taryn. This was not something that I had been praying about. I didn't know how to interpret what was just spoken to me. When service dismissed, I went to the prophet and asked her for clarity. She couldn't really give me any. She said that was all God gave her. I kind of alluded to the fact that having a baby wasn't on my to-do list at the moment and I would have preferred a prophecy telling me that my millions were coming in a few days. She didn't change her prophecy. My family that was at church at the time of the prophecy started getting excited and congratulating me on the baby to come. I still was trying to accept the prophecy. After a discussion with my husband, we decided to go ahead and try to have a baby. We had the go ahead from God saying we "owed" him another. We were married, had our own home, decent jobs and was still young enough to add a 3rd child to our home. Over the course of the next year, I became obsessed with having a baby. I started reading baby magazines. I trolled pregnancy websites. I had multiple girl and boy names that I was contemplating naming my next offspring. Godparents were picked out. I even god a minivan for the anticipated arrival of our new baby. We did EVERYTHING we knew how to do and even some things we didn't know how to do in order to get pregnant. Nothing happened. For a year, nothing happened. The books and websites say that a healthy couple should get pregnant within a year. It didn't happen that way for us. Of course I started questioning God. "Why did you tell me I owed you another kid if you won't let me get pregnant?" I started feeling some type of way. I had faith to believe. I was applying works to my faith. I mean we practiced the "works" almost every day! Where was my baby? My husband and I went in for fertility testing. We confirmed that his soldiers were matching strong and in formation. I was in good shape, but I blamed myself. Why couldn't I get pregnant? We saw a fertility specialist and I began taking fertility medications. I had countless appointments, various exams, scans and procedures. Even with the fertility medication, I still could not get pregnant. It was just too much emotionally and physically. Trying to get pregnant even affected my spiritual life. I couldn't pray because I was sort of ticked with God for not cooperating with me. And if I heard one more person say, "Relax, it will happen." Or "Trust God" I was going to sucker punch someone in the face. This process went on for almost 2 years. 2 years of trying and failing. 2 years of seeing other women get pregnant. 2 years of hearing other babies with the names I had picked out for my child. 2 years of buying baby items in faith, with no baby to show for it. 2 years and nothing. I had stopped the fertility medication because it wasn't working. I was emotionally overwhelmed. Somewhere around the end of the 2 year mark, as I was cleaning the house, it dawned on me that my period was late. I didn't get excited because I had taken a pregnancy test at least 20 times in the past 2 years. They were all negative. I wasn't expecting this one to be any different. To my shock and surprise, this pregnancy test was positive! I could not believe it. I took another test to be sure. That one was positive too! Thank you Jesus!!!!!! Finally!!!!!!!!!!! OMG!!!!!!!!!!!! Everything I had been through in the past 2 years didn't even matter anymore. I was finally pregnant. That Sunday at church, I danced all around the building. My friends that knew I was pregnant held the usher circle around me for my safety, but I didn't need them. I was ecstatic. I was extremely happy. I was on cloud nine for weeks.

About 3 weeks later, I woke up bleeding. I went to my doctor's office. After an exam. I was informed that I was miscarrying and there was nothing that could be done to save my baby. Devastated cannot describe how I felt. I went home to bleed for the next couple of days. God why did you make me wait 2 years to get pregnant and then take my baby away from me? I went from the highest of highs to the lowest of lows. I did not want to talk to anyone, go to church, or do anything. I was crushed. The bleeding stopped after a few days and life had to continue. I just gave up. I didn't care what God said anymore. I was done. I felt like a fool. I felt like God lied. It was hard to move on from that pain and disappointment. I named it and claimed it. I had a prophecy to confirm it and the faith to match it, but the end result was not what I wanted nor what I expected.

To add insult to injury, a couple of weeks later, I was lying in bed and felt like I peed on myself. I got up and went to the bathroom and when I looked down I saw what looked like a crime scene. I was hemorrhaging. The sight of blood made me weak. My husband lined the car seat in garbage bags and rushed me towards the hospital. The ambulance met us half way there. I arrive at the hospital and learn that my earlier miscarriage was not complete. I was losing my baby all over again. I had to have a D&C and spend the night in the hospital. I had to grieve my baby all over again.

This particular test/trial or whatever you want to call it was difficult for me. I decided to call it quits with trying to have a baby. The emotional roller coaster wrecked my mind and spirit. I decided to work on rebuilding my spiritual life because it was injured.

A couple of months later, I learned by surprise that my brother had fathered a baby boy. He was not aware of the baby until he was about 9 months old. Initially it was a slap in my face. Here is someone else who wasn't even trying to get pregnant is having a baby. Nevertheless, this was my nephew and I was going to love him. When I first saw him, I fell in love. He looked exactly like my brother did at that age. Over the course of months and years and various events.....my husband and I started taking care of my nephew more and more. Spending the weekend with us turned into staying the week and that turned into months. My nephew, Elijah, eventually moved in with my husband and me. He is our 3rd child together.

Lesson: The word came to me that I owed God another child. I never sought God for specific instructions or clarity. I just took what I heard and ran with it. I created a plan. It was a good plan. I put it into action and expected God to get on board. He never did. My emotions dictated my relationship with God. My will super ceded his will. I couldn't hear God because I was too busy planning my life and putting my plan into effect. God was speaking, I just wasn't listening....even rebuking him, claiming he was the devil. Silly me. After Elijah became a huge part of our lives, God let me know that I owing him another child meant that we needed to be available and willing to raise another child that we did not create. If God asked me to do that previously, in all honesty, I would have said no. Even after Elijah came into our lives, I still struggled with raising someone else's child simply because I didn't want to mess him up. I did not want to be responsible for him if he turned out for the worse by being with me.

I had only considered my way to get things done. I had a "word" from the Lord, but I didn't listen long enough for the details, plan and process for that word to manifest itself. God may have very well been speaking to me through the process, but I was not listening. He may not have said a word to me at all because I didn't stop to ask him for direction. Sometimes, if we are so full of ourselves, God won't speak because he knows we are not listening and we wouldn't receive what he has to say. Don't act like you haven't told God no. I don't recommend it, but I did do it. I now believe that God allowed me to go through that entire process, as heart wrenching as it was, to show me that he knows what's best for me. I thought I knew. There have been many times I tried to talk God out of having me do certain things that I am not comfortable with or just did not want to do. He knows how stubborn I am. He also knows how to break me down to get my attention. He knows how to remind me to be still and know that he is God and that he will never put more on me than I can bare. He also knows that he cannot give me a lot of details at once because I will try to incorporate my will into his and that never works. I know I frustrate the Lord when I try to alter his will to fit my emotions and insecurities at that particular time. He withheld the details from me for over 2 years because I was not in the place to accept his plan. We often miss seeing the bigger picture. It really doesn't matter if the Lord gives us a play by play, fully detailed thesis on his plan for us or if he simply just whispers a few simple words to us. He just wants us to trust him and his plan. Point blank. When we fully surrender to Christ that means we accept what his will is for our lives. We don't try to make him change it to accommodate us. We work at changing our self to accommodate him. It really is a simple concept: Surrender to God. Trust him. Be obedient. Blessings occur. What complicates this concept most of the time is our emotions and need to be in control of everything. Control and untamed emotions are a bad combination. God doesn't work in emotions, he works in faith. Don't allow your emotions to separate you from God and his will for your life.

Scriptures:

Proverbs 10:22New King James Version (NKJV)

²² The blessing of the LORD makes one rich, And He adds no sorrow with it.

> If your crying over it…..repeatedly….then maybe it shouldn't be considered a blessing.

Psalm 42:11New Living Translation (NLT)

¹¹ Why am I discouraged? Why is my heart so sad? I will put my hope in God! I will praise him again— my Savior and my God!

> Being overly emotional is a sign that your hope may be displaced. Reset your hope with praise and remembering who your Savior is.

Philippians 4:6-7New Living Translation (NLT)

⁶ Don't worry about anything; instead, pray about everything. Tell God what you need, and thank him for all he has done. ⁷ Then you will experience God's peace, which exceeds anything we can understand. His peace will guard your hearts and minds as you live in Christ Jesus.

> Follow the above listed steps: 1.) Stop worrying (allowing your emotions to take over). 2.) Make the decision to pray about everything specifically (don't forget to listen). 3.) Thank God for everything, even those things that you haven't seen. 4.) Accept HIS peace which will super cede your emotions and keep you calm.

Consider This: Who has the most control in your life? Your emotions or God? You cannot serve two masters. Pick a side.

Interrogation Time: Ask yourself these tough questions. Be honest. Write your answers down and begin to pray for God to help you to keep your emotions under subjection.

1.) How has your emotions dictated various areas of your life?

2.) Why are you experiencing anxiety, depression and emotional highs and lows in your relationship with God?

3.) How do you handle disappointment when God does not answer your request the way that you want him to? How do you recover from disappointment?

_____
_____
_____
_____
_____
_____
_____
_____
_____
_____
_____
_____
_____
_____
_____

Chapter 9:

Insufficient Funds and Overdraft Fees

We all have things that we are not proud of in our pasts. Some secrets I will share. Other secrets will go to the grave with me. On my list, of things I don't brag about is the fact that I have had 2 abortions. I knew that God was not pleased with my decision or how I got in the predicament in the first place. I chose to have the abortions because I felt that I was not ready to become a mother. I looked at my situation and saw that I was not prepared. Becoming a mother was a challenge. It was scary. I knew I would be judged as a single mother. I would disappointment my family. I was a preacher's kid, so that would bring shame on my parents too. I knew that my life would not be about me anymore. I would become responsible for someone other than myself and to be honest, I wasn't doing that great a job looking after me. I wasn't mature. I was not an expert in the field of parenting. I was still living home with my parents, so that meant I would need their help but they were not obligated to help me. I had a part time job, but becoming a parent would require me to get a full time job in order to support my child. I could not be certain that the father of the baby was going to help me. Was he going to stick around? I really didn't know. I couldn't hang out with my friends as much anymore because I would have to take care of my baby. If I carried a baby to term, I would get fat. I would be in discomfort due to my body changing. And let's not even talk about labor! I could barely handle monthly cramps, I knew contractions would probably end my life. Every story I had heard about labor was torturous. There were complications and issues. Bottom line: I just was not ready to have a baby, so I terminated my pregnancy. I ended it. I made a life altering decision regarding my life. I have had to live with the consequences of my decision.

Lesson: Decades later, the Lord use the abortions I had as a teachable moment for me. I made the decision to have an abortion because I was afraid and unprepared for life with a baby. The Lord showed me that at the time of the abortion, my feelings could be validated, but not once did I ask him for help or consider his plan for the pregnancy. There are dreams, visions and assignments that God gives us. Most of the time, these assignments do not occur when life is going good and we are being an A+ Christian. Every assignment, task, dream or vision that the Lord has given me has always come at the most inconvenient time. I would pray and ask God for certain things or I would pray and say God whatever you want me to do I will do it. When the Lord would bring it to past or it was my time to go forth, I often aborted my mission. I looked at my circumstances. I was not ready. I did not see the resources that I thought I needed in order to be successful. The mission would cause my life to change significantly. I would have to give up my agenda. My personal thoughts and ideas had to be put on hold while I took care of the mission. I would count up my personal cost. I would see what I would have to sacrifice and then ultimately decide to terminate. It was just too much. I would get overwhelmed with what I thought I would be losing. I would probably lose friends. I would probably lose my freedom. I wouldn't have the support system in place that I wanted. I knew it would cause me to become uncomfortable because it was something new. I was inexperienced. I saw others that were going down a similar path that the Lord was commissioning me to go down. I saw their struggles and that was a red flag to me. I was making decisions about what I would and would not do when asked of the Lord to go forth. I would shut the Lord down. I would end the assignment before it even got started. I would consider the sacrifices I would have to make and not go through with it. The Lord spoke to me and told me about all the missions and assignments from him I aborted because I did not trust him. That's the simple truth. I had not fully surrendered to him. Every time he told me to do something, I considered it based upon my own strength and resources. I did not consider that even though my feelings and thoughts were valid, he is the one who would have carried me through each task. I would abort opportunities to minister because I did not want to bring attention to myself. I would terminate assignments that caused me to get out of my comfort zone because I did not enjoy being uncomfortable. I would delay my response to go higher in God because I knew the higher I went, the more demons I would have to deal with. No thank you God. Whenever God would require more of me for the kingdom I would abort the mission. I continued to consider me and my capabilities. I didn't think about him or his resources. I didn't consider that if he called me to do something, he will also equip me to do it. I didn't consider that he would not leave me or forsake me. I knew we have to suffer for his sake, but I wasn't thinking about the reward on the other side. I saw the suffering and ran the other way. It was not fear that caused me to say no. It was the unknown that caused me to say no. I didn't want to lose myself in the process. I did not want to become the thing that I dreaded; a failure. When the Lord showed this to me, I had to ask for forgiveness. There were so many things that I did not do because they were an inconvenience. Simple as that. I asked God to help me not to tell him no anymore. What a prayer to pray! Has he asked me to do things since I prayed that prayer? Yes. Did I say no? Yes…..but the things I have said no to, I have gone back to the Lord and asked him to help me to turn that quick no into a slow yes. He is still working on me. When he leads me, I may be thinking no…but my spirit is saying "ok Lord, I am your vessel and use me how you see fit." My assignments now are not without difficulty. The things that I was concerned about occurring have occurred. But they were not as bad as I anticipated. He has given me what I needed every step of the way. I often do not know the end result, but I know I am doing what he wants me to do. Understand this, we should be knowledgeable about things and count up the cost prior to doing anything. We should not be naïve or haphazardly approach assignments. We have to make sure God is calling us to that direction. We have to make sure that our faith and trust is in him and not in ourselves or our resources.

Scriptures:

2 Timothy 3:16,17 NKJV

All Scripture is given by inspiration of God, and is profitable for doctrine, for reproof, for correction, for instruction in righteousness, that the man of God may be equipped for every good work.

> God's word will give us what we need to be equipped for our assignment.

Romans 8:30, 31 KJV

Moreover whom he did predestinate, them he also called: and whom he called, them he also justified: and whom he justified, them he also glorified. What shall we then say to these things? If God be for us, who can be against us?

You have God's full support when you do it his way.

Proverbs 29:18 KJV

Where there is no vision, the people perish...

Aborting the vision and assignment will lead to many different types of death.

Consider This: The reward is far greater than the struggle and sacrifice.

Interrogation Time: Ask yourself these tough questions, Be honest. Write your answers down and begin to pray for God to help you refrain from aborting future assignments and missions.

1.) Think of an assignment or mission that you aborted. What made you abort prior to giving birth to that assignment?

2.) Think of an assignment of mission that you birthed. What made you proceed with the birthing process and not abort?

3.) How can you prevent aborting future assignments?

Chapter 10:

#RelationshipGoals

My husband Terrence and I were married February 1998. One of the best days of my life. Weddings are great. They bring family and friends together and celebrate Love. Weddings are fun. You dance, smile, eat, drink and be merry from start to finish. Marriages are a different story. People will take months and years to plan the perfect wedding. A lot of times that same effort and enthusiasm is not put forth in planning marriage. Marriage is beautiful and great. It is a wonderful union of two becoming one. Let me tell you though, that this becoming one does not occur when vows are pledged. Marriage takes work. If anyone tells you that marriage is easy, they are lying to your face. Don't get me wrong, I am happily married and I would marry Terry Todd all over again in another life if I had to. But what I did not know is that after the wedding is when the real work would begin. Merging two people into one is quite a task. We can do all things through Christ, who gives us strength and trust me, you will need his strength if you want to remain in a loving and healthy marriage.

During a particular season in our marriage, I felt that Terrence was not communicating with me how I needed him to communicate. I also felt that he was not showing me the affection that I desired. He was in the midst of starting his own business and he was really busy. I was feeling neglected and left out. I wanted us to be close. I wanted us to be besties. I wanted to feel that connection. I wanted all the things that make a relationship great. I wanted that story book fairy tale. Don't we all? I would tell him how I felt, but things did not change to my satisfaction. We barely spoke. If we did speak it was about household issues and the kids. He slept on his side of the bed, I slept on my side of the bed. We were more like roommates than husband and wife. We weren't really arguing or fighting. We were basically co-habituating. The scary part of this was that we had gotten comfortable in this season. We barely had any intimacy between us. We would talk about making things better, but barely put in the work to change our situation. The relationship with your spouse requires maintenance in order to run smoothly. Most of us take our vehicle to get an oil change and serviced routinely. Once a year you have to get an inspection on the vehicle. Marriage requires constant maintenance services, oil changes and fill ups. If we are not careful, we can allow marriage or our spouse to feel like another chore that needs to get done that we really don't want to do. My husband and I had allowed our marriage to get to that point. I wanted more from him, I loved him, but he wasn't giving me what I felt I needed. He felt the same way. Thoughts of divorce occurred.

I prayed that God would help us, but it seemed like nothing changed. I just wanted my husband to show me that he loved me. I just wanted to feel some passion between us. I just wanted to be acknowledged. I just wanted some quality time. I just wanted to feel like I was important to him and a priority. He wanted the same from me, but neither of us were making that effort. We were waiting on the other to make the first move but neither of us was willing to initiate the process of admitting our wrong doings and then finding the solutions to make things better.

One day, I had enough of Terrence being cold towards me. I was not going to take it anymore. I was not going to be played or treated as if I didn't matter. My eyes were full of tears and I cried out to God. I was done. I couldn't live like this anymore. I was venting to God and letting him know all the things that Terrence had done wrong. I was going in on my husband to God. I got it all out and guess what? No response from God. I don't know what I was expecting him to say, but I did not feel any different or had any direction after I cried out to him. I was devastated and disappointed yet again. The next morning, Terrence got up from bed to get dressed for work. I was awake and just lying in bed. He didn't say good morning, he didn't acknowledge me and continued getting dressed. Tears were rolling out my eyes, but I did not let him see them. He grabbed his keys and was walking out the bedroom. I decided to be petty and further prove my point that he was the worst person on earth by saying "Well good morning to you too!" He turned around and said good morning and walked out the room. I shook my head and cried a little bit more.

Lesson: I told you earlier that I was not one that heard the Lord speak with a loud voice from heaven. But on this particular morning, I heard him speak to my heart clearly. He said to me "Wanda, the way you say Terrence is treating you, is the same way you are treating me." My heart dropped. I couldn't move. I was in shock. My heart is palpitating as I am writing this right now because I remember that moment so clearly. I was so ashamed. I couldn't argue with God. He was right. I couldn't plead my case. He was right. I couldn't smooth it over. He was right. I couldn't put the blame on Terrence. God was right. The very things I complained about were the very things I was guilty of. The relationship goals that I wanted to obtain with my husband, God wanted to obtain with me. That morning that I begrudgingly spoke to Terrence and said Good morning, his response to me was an afterthought. Whenever I communicated with God during that season was an afterthought. God rewinded the tape and pointed out to me how I had neglected my relationship with him. I did not have meaningful communication with him. I neglected him. I did not have any passion for Christ. I was not building an intimate relationship with him. He was an afterthought. I was busy with church work, my family, my career, my friends, my anything else. My relationship with God was not on my list of priorities. I am being honest. I was going to church but my relationship was pretty nonexistent. Yes, I would sing and shout and go to 20 services a week, but I did not share any intimacy with my Savior. As I was waiting for my husband to spend time with me, make me feel wanted and needed and like a priority, God was waiting on the same thing from me.

In marriage, when you get to a stale point you really cannot remember how you got there and how long you have been there. If you sit down and think about it for a while, it may come to you. You often don't realize how bad things are until you are in a bad place.

How could I ask God to restore and fix my husband when I wasn't asking him to restore and fix me? I had to repent. I did not realize the level of neglect that I had inflicted on my relationship with God. Just as I desired a closer relationship with my husband, my Savior desired a closer relationship with me. He wanted to hear me say "I Love you". He wanted me to set aside my "busy work" and make him a part of my day, every day. He looked forward to fellowshipping with me and I had cheated him out of that opportunity time and time again. He wanted my pure worship and praise without distraction. He also wanted me to want him. He wanted me to show that I wanted him.

When we are having difficulties in relationships with others, let us evaluate ourselves first. It is easy to point out the other person's flaws or make theirs seem so much bigger than ours.

I repented to God and I also repented to my husband. I had a long honest talk with God and with my husband. I confessed my faults and desperately wanted to do anything I needed to do to fix both relationships. It took time and work. Today, both relationships are so much better.

God wants to be and has to be number 1. He has to be on top of the priority list. It is fairly easy to allow the most important relationship you have to dwindle and fade to black if you are not putting in the effort to maintain daily. God doesn't want to be a pen pal or in a long distance relationship with you. He wants daily intimacy and communication. He is not going to force you to service and maintain your relationship with him. He wants you to want him just as much as he wants you. To him, you were simply to die for. He has proven his love to you, now it's time to prove your love to him.

Scripture:

Deuteronomy 7:9 New King James Version (NKJV)

[9] *"Therefore know that the Lord your God, He is God, the faithful God who keeps covenant and mercy for a thousand generations with those who love Him and keep His commandments;*

> God will do his part in the relationship, you must commit to doing yours.

1 John 1:3,4 New King James Version (NKJV)

³ that which we have seen and heard we declare to you, that you also may have fellowship with us; and truly our fellowship is with the Father and with His Son Jesus Christ. ⁴ And these things we write to you that your joy may be full.

> Fellowship (relationship) with the Lord brings joy. If you Joy is not full, maybe there is a problem in the relationship.

Zephaniah 3:17New Living Translation (NLT)

¹⁷ For the LORD your God is living among you. He is a mighty savior. He will take delight in you with gladness. With his love, he will calm all your fears‧ He will rejoice over you with joyful songs."

> He will keep you calm and at peace. He wants to be the lover of your soul. He is so in love with you that he sings love songs about you. He had love on his mind when he died for you.

Consider This: If you have ever had your heart break, you know it is one of the most devastating experiences in the world. You find it hard to accept that someone you have done so much for, sacrificed for, and showed so much love to could hurt you so bad. We do the same thing to our Savior when we abandon our relationship with him.

Interrogation Time: Ask yourself these tough questions, be honest. Write your answers down and begin to pray for God to help you evaluate your current relationship status and goals with him. Ask him to help you make the necessary adjustments.

Are you content with God as your pen pal? Do you enjoy a long distance relationship with him? You can change your relationship status with him, but it begins with you.

1.) In what ways have you deserted or abandoned your relationship with God?

2.) Why do you want to be in a relationship with God? What are your relationship goals?

3.) What are the similarities and differences in the relationships you have with God and others? Who gets the better parts of you? Why?

4.) How can you improve your relationship with God?

_____

_____

_____

_____

_____

Conclusion

One thing I had to honestly ask myself was this: Do you want to hear what God is saying? I had to answer this question truthfully. There were times in my life that I did not want to hear God because I already knew what his answer would be. I knew I was in the wrong and I did not want to be corrected yet. I was in relationships with men that I knew I should not have been in. I was participating in activities that I knew God was not pleased with. I was violating my temple in many different ways. I did not have to pray about these things. I did not have to fast for an answer. I knew what God was saying through his word, but I choose not to listen and obey. There have been times that I have heard from God, but I did not want to do what he said. I did not want to become who he wanted me to be. I would go into self-sabotage mode. I would just start purposely sinning. I know that sounds crazy, and it is crazy. I would attempt to disqualify myself by proving how unworthy and unrighteous I was so that he would use someone more qualified than me. I would do things that I knew God did not approve of because I did not want to listen to him and his word.

I had to come to myself and make a decision. Did I want to continue playing with God and my life? Was my stubbornness leading to me a place that I could not come back from? How many more times was I going to grieve God with my shenanigans? I had to decide that I was going to be obedient and seek God with my heart and not my flesh. I had to remember that I was created for his glory and purpose. I had to understand that this life is not mine. Sure, I could be reckless and do whatever I want to do, but at what cost. I decided that yielding to his will and voice was a much better option.

I have shared personal examples of how God has spoken to me through the years. I was looking for him to communicate with me in one way. He chose to use my everyday life issues to teach me a lesson and show me who he is. How did I recognize God communicating with me in each of these situations? I started to listen….without distractions.

Learn self-control – You cannot be all over the place and unfocused when communicating with God. Learn how to have quiet time with him by blocking out all distractions. Don't bring your phone into your fellowship time with him. That is the number one distraction. A text message or some type of alert will always grab your attention when you are trying to listen.

Make time with the Lord a priority – Why would he want to speak with you if he is an afterthought? Make sure it is quality time. When I see my husband making an effort to spend time with me, it makes my day and night! Set your alarm to wake up at least 30 minutes earlier so that you can start your day off communicating with him. When you plan your week full of activities, put him on your calendar. Keep that appointment! Do whatever you need to do to make him a priority. Make reading the bible a priority as well. His word tells you everything you need to know about him. You can find examples of how he communicated with others in the bible as well.

Be Honest – If you are struggling with an issue, be honest with God. Why try to hide it? He already knows. Pride will put a wedge between you and God. When you are upset with him, tell him!!! Vent to him. Holler, scream, and yell if you need to. Just get it out! He can work and communicate with you when you don't have all the answers figured out.

Remove Limits – Stop putting God in a box. Again, he communicates in various ways. You may pass a billboard sign that resonates with your spirt. A commercial can bring you to tears and minister to your heart. A 4 year old can give you a word from heaven hot off the press. A scripture that you have read since childhood can one day have an entirely different meaning just when you need it. Open your mind and heart to receive from God in more than one way. How can you be sure it is him speaking? Whatever is said or interpreted will line up with his word. It will bring peace and correction. If you are unsure if it is really God speaking to you, ask for clarity and direction. The more time you spend with him and in his word, you will question him speaking less and less.

Expect him to speak – Why pray or talk to God if you really don't expect him to respond? He wants to talk to you. He is in love with you. He enjoys your company. He looks forward to communicating with you. At times he will be silent for his own purposes, at certain times. But he will always reassure you of his love for you and desire to have an intimate relationship with you.

Write it down – Start writing in a journal. I know not everyone likes to write, but it is very beneficial and therapeutic. I have journals from years ago. At times, I go back and read what I have written. When I made those journal entries, I was seeking answers from God that I didn't have at the time. When I reviewed them, I was able to recall how God answered my prayer, spoke to my heart, corrected me and ministered to me. I was able to recall ways that he communicated to me without parting the Heavens and yelling from above.

Don't give up – Change or improvements do not happen overnight. Satan will have you thinking that your plan to do better is not working. He is a liar! Just because you do not see instant results does not mean you are a failure. I promise that when you commit to prioritize your relationship with God, all sorts of crap is going to come your way to get you off focus. Expect it. But don't you dare give up. I had committed to making 7-8pm my time with the Lord. Dinner would be done and I would have finished tending to the family by 7pm. This time commitment did not last long. This did not work for me the way I had hoped. The family wanted my attention. I was tired from work; something on TV would catch my attention. I didn't give up and say oh well I tried. I had to re-evaluate myself and set a time that would bring the least if any distractions. I switched to the early morning hours, before anyone else woke up at home. Now it was not easy getting out of my bed and I missed hitting the snooze button, but I knew I had to make him a priority. I knew starting my day with him would be the best thing for me. I did not give up. I just had to come up with a better plan.

Final Thoughts

God is always speaking to us. He may not use his James Earl Jones voice that comes with a thunder from Heaven, but he is always talking. Due to his great love for us, he has opened up the doors of communication and speaks to us in many ways. He will communicate with us through his word, in nature, miraculous acts and various other areas. One way that we miss God communicating with us is in our day to day operations. In the easy and not so easy lessons of life, our father is always speaking to us. The question to be answered is are we listening?

Why go through trials and tribulations and not gain something from them? Are you able to hear God or is your mind cluttered with your own agenda, plans or other distractions? Are you repeating lessons in your life because you are not listening? Have you missed the blessings from your lessons? Did you miss the answer to your prayers? Learn to recognize and embrace when the Father has something to say to you. He will use whatever he desires to get your attention. Understand your Heavenly Father's voice and learn he communicates with you in more ways than one.

About the Author

LaWanda Cheryelle Todd is a minister, writer, and now officially a published author. She has a Bachelor's Degree in Human Services/Management and has been working in the HIV community for over 15 years.

She enjoys adventures and trying new things. She loves to laugh as well as spend time with her family. LaWanda's bubbly personality brings great joy to anyone who enters her presence.

LaWanda is a native of New Haven, Connecticut and currently lives in Greenville, NC with her husband and children.